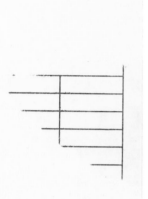

I Bet You Didn't Know That...

THERE ARE GOLF
BALLS ON THE MOON

and Other Facts and Curiosities

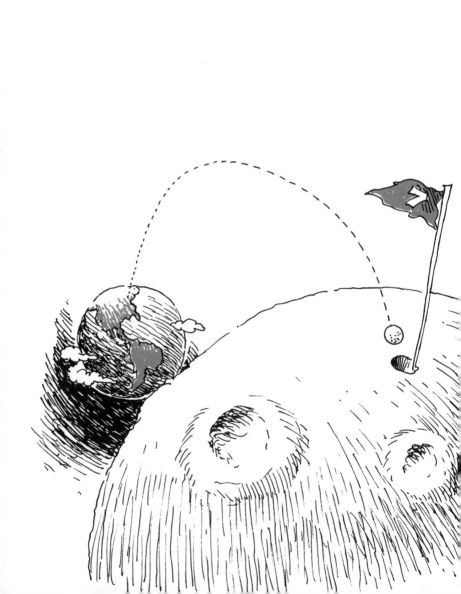

I Bet You Didn't Know That...

THERE ARE GOLF BALLS ON THE MOON

and Other Facts and Curiosities

by Carol Iverson • pictures by Jack Lindstrom

 Lerner Publications Company • Minneapolis

With thanks to Gary DeGrote and his sixth graders,
Addi Engen, Isabel Marvin, Joan Ennis, Torild
Homstad, and my husband, Art

Library of Congress Cataloging-in-Publication Data

Iverson, Carol.
  There are golf balls on the moon and other facts and curiosities /
Carol Iverson ; pictures by Jack Lindstrom.
     p.   cm. – (I bet you didn't know that)
  Summary: Presents a variety of facts about history, sports, and
people.
    ISBN 0-8225-2275-6 (lib. bdg.)
    1. Curiosities and wonders – Juvenile literature. [1. Curiosities
and wonders.] I. Lindstrom, Jack, ill. II. Title. III. Series: Iverson,
Carol. I bet you didn't know that.
AG243.I84   1990
030 – dc20   89-27185
                                                                 CIP
                                                                  AC

1 2 3 4 5 6 7 8 9 10 99 98 97 96 95 94 93 92 91 90

I Bet You Didn't Know That...

The first clock was built around 1360 and was off by about two hours every day.

Early watches had only one hand, which indicated the hour.

I Bet You Didn't Know That...

In 1957, muscleman Paul Anderson lifted more than 6,000 pounds with his back.

To prepare for war, some North American Indians played a game of lacrosse with as many as 500 men on a side.

In 1938, Australian golfer Stanley Gard played 250 holes in one day.

The first badminton birdie was made of a cork that was stuck with feathers.

The longest boxing match was between Andy Bowen and Jack Burke and took place in New Orleans in 1893. The fight lasted more than 7 hours and was declared a draw after 110 rounds.

I Bet You Didn't Know That...

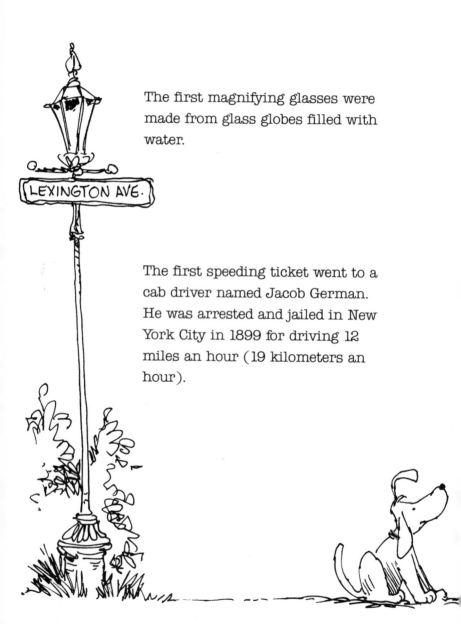

The first magnifying glasses were made from glass globes filled with water.

The first speeding ticket went to a cab driver named Jacob German. He was arrested and jailed in New York City in 1899 for driving 12 miles an hour (19 kilometers an hour).

LEXINGTON AVE.

The first Ferris wheel had 36 cars that each held
60 passengers for a total of 2,160 riders.

The first skyscraper was built in Chicago in 1885.
It was ten stories tall.

I Bet You Didn't Know That...

Tchaikovsky's career was financed by a woman he never met.

Wolfgang Mozart was composing music when he was five years old.

The composer Beethoven began to lose his hearing at age 28 and was totally deaf by age 50. He continued to compose but never heard his later works performed.

The Earl of Sandwich invented the sandwich so he could eat while he was gambling.

I Bet You Didn't Know That...

The game of horseshoes is thought to have originated in Roman army camps about 100 A.D.

During a game of jai alai, the ball can reach a speed of 160 miles an hour (256 km/h).

In 1457, golf was banned in Scotland because it interfered with archery, a national defense program.

I Bet You Didn't Know That...

The first photograph was taken in 1826. It took eight hours to expose the picture.

All of Leonardo Da Vinci's notes were written backwards.

Leonardo Da Vinci spent about three years painting the Mona Lisa.

It took Michelangelo about four years to paint the ceiling of the Sistine Chapel.

I Bet You Didn't Know That...

According to some scientists, the first rainstorm lasted hundreds of years.

One of the first zoos belonged to Queen Hath-shepsut of Egypt in about 1500 B.C.

The Romans played a game similar to golf, using a leather ball stuffed with feathers.

Hundreds of years ago in Germany, people bowled in churches. A strike was considered a sign of a righteous life.

Balls and pins found in Egyptian tombs show that bowling is about 7,000 years old.

I Bet You Didn't Know That...

The Roman emperor Caligula once made his horse a senator.

The first horses in America were brought from Europe by Hernando Cortez in 1519.

Some pigs have been trained to retrieve game just as hunting dogs do.

George Washington was the only U.S. president who did not live in the White House.

The first U.S. president to fly in an airplane was Theodore Roosevelt, in 1910.

The first airline stewardess was hired in 1930 to care for passengers and help push planes in and out of hangars, among other things.

I Bet You Didn't Know That...

Benjamin Franklin suggested setting clocks ahead an hour for daylight saving time as a joke.

Ben Franklin drew the first newspaper cartoon in the American colonies in 1754.

Queen Elizabeth I owned at least 300 gowns and 100 wigs in her lifetime.

Thomas Edison patented 1,093 inventions in his lifetime.

George Custer became a general when he was only 23.

Christopher Columbus never set foot on what is now the continental United States.

Diamond Jim Brady's average dinner consisted of two or three dozen oysters, six crabs, two bowls of soup, six lobsters, two ducks, a sirloin steak, and dessert.

I Bet You Didn't Know That...

The first movie in an airplane was shown in 1929.

The first telephone message was Alexander Graham Bell's call for help after he spilled acid on his clothing.

The first telephone directory was made for New Haven, Connecticut, in 1878. It had about 50 names.

The first color television transmission was made on July 3, 1928, in London, England.

The first president to appear on television was Franklin D. Roosevelt, in 1939.

Radio pioneer Mary Somerville said, "Television won't last. It's a flash in the pan."

I Bet You Didn't Know That

George Washington's false teeth
were hinged together in the back
with springs.

The original salary for the president
of the United States was $25,000
a year.

President James Garfield could write
with both hands at the same time.
Some say he could write a different
language with each hand.

The White House was originally gray. The mansion was burned during the War of 1812. When it was rebuilt after the war, it was painted white to hide the smoke stains.

President Andrew Johnson never attended school.

William Henry Harrison was president of the United States for only a month.

I Bet You Didn't Know That...

In 1950, South African boxer Vic Toweel downed Englishman Danny O'Sullivan 14 times in 10 rounds.

In 1935, track-and-field star Jesse Owens broke three world records and tied a fourth within 45 minutes.

The Cleveland Indians baseball team used to be called the Cleveland Spiders.

American football was played with 15 men on a team until 1880.

The first intercollegiate baseball game was held on July 1, 1859. Amherst beat Williams, 73 to 32, in a game that lasted 3½ hours.

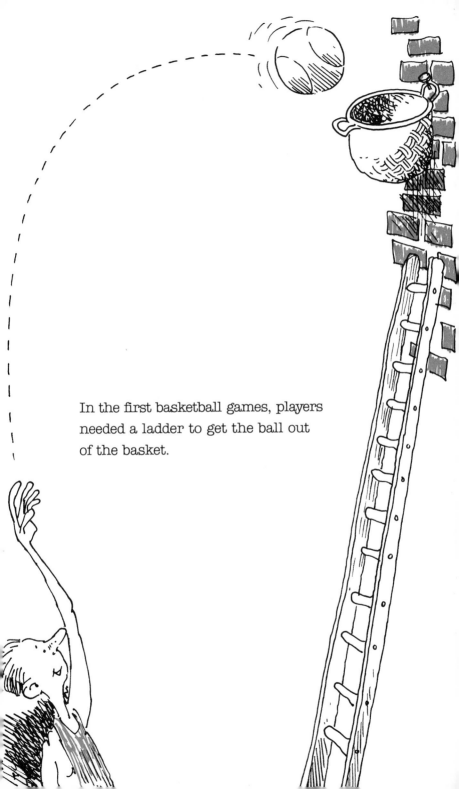

In the first basketball games, players needed a ladder to get the ball out of the basket.

I Bet You Didn't Know That...

Francis Scott Key wrote *The Star-Spangled Banner* on the back of an envelope.

During World War II, a bomb missed Leonardo Da Vinci's painting, *The Last Supper,* by only a few yards.

Women could serve in the United States Congress before they had the right to vote in national elections.

The first adhesive postage stamps in the United States were made in 1842.

The first blue jeans were made for gold miners in California in 1850.

The first handshakes were not a sign of friendship.
The handshake was used to see if another person
was carrying a weapon.

I Bet You Didn't Know That...

The first pencil with an eraser was patented in 1858.

The first phonograph recording was made in 1877 when Thomas Edison recited "Mary had a little lamb" into the phonograph.

From 1890 to 1911, the city of Pittsburgh, by government decree, was told to drop the "h" from its name.

When the Golden Gate Bridge was being built in the 1930s, any construction worker who showed up with a hangover was given a big dose of sauerkraut juice.

The last cavalry charge took place in 1941, during World War II, when Mongolian horsemen charged a German infantry division near Moscow. About 2,000 cavalrymen died in the attack, but not a single German died.

There are golf balls on the moon. Alan Shepard was the first astronaut to play golf on the moon when Apollo 14 landed in 1971.

About the Author

Carol Iverson has been collecting interesting facts and trivia for the **I Bet You Didn't Know That** books for many years. Formerly a dental assistant, Iverson now spends much of her time writing for children. She lives in Northfield, Minnesota, with her husband, Art.

About the Artist

Artist **Jack Lindstrom** is a native of Minneapolis and a partner in a Minneapolis art studio. Lindstrom graduated from the Minneapolis College of Art and Design and currently illustrates a syndicated comic strip for United Features.